Hidden Bottles

The Chronicles of an (Ex) Co-Dependent

Ellaina Nicholette Dolater

Hidden Bottles

The Chronicles of an (Ex) Co-Dependent

Ellaina Nicholette Dolater

TYRO Publishing Services

Hidden Bottles
The Chronicles of an (Ex) Co-Dependent

TYRO Publishing: Conroe, Texas http://tyropublishing.com/

Cover Artwork design in partnership with TNT Publishing

For inquiries please contact the author
in writing via email (Attention: Jswilson1969@gmail.com)

All scripture used from
The Holy Bible King James Version in The Public Domain.

Printed in the United States of America First Printing, 2016

ISBN-13: 978-1542979627
ISBN-10: 1542979625

Dedication

In loving memory of Imelda Manzanarez
-Our Champion and Hero

To Patricia Wells, my baby sister.

Special Thanks to Robin Holloway.

Thanks to Vi Cooper.

Glory to God most of all.

Jesus saith unto him, I am the way, the truth, and the life: no man cometh unto the Father, but by me. John 14:6 King James Version

Acknowledgment

This book describes the author's painful struggles growing up in an alcoholic household while giving the reader hope as the author also outlines her path to self-healing--a compelling read for anyone seeking relief from the traumas caused by an alcoholic parent. Best wishes!!!

– Dr. Koppersmith

Contents

Introduction

Ellaina has had a personal experience witnessing domestic violence first hand growing up and seeing it as a young child with her mother and sibling being abused. Ellaina also had two sisters that died of alcohol abuse and left young children and devastated siblings behind.

This personal experience in her life gave her an up close experience in understanding the cycle to better understand God's healing inside and out and how to break this endless cycle that can be rooted in your family.

Your family and future generations can have a life out of bondage in knowing the truth of what Christ did on the cross and give the devil a black eye once and for all!

CHAPTER ONE

Alcoholism Hurts Families

Noah, a farmer, was the first to plant a vineyard. He drank from its wine, got drunk and passed out, naked in his tent. Ham, the father of Canaan, saw that his father was naked and told his two brothers who were outside the tent. Shem and Japheth took a cloak, held it between them from their shoulders, walked backward and covered their father's nakedness, keeping their faces turned away so they did not see their father's exposed body. (The MSG Bible)

The Bible shares the account of Noah's family after the flood.

And Noah began to be an husbandman, and he planted a vineyard: And he drank of the wine, and was drunken; and he was uncovered within his tent. And Ham, the father of Canaan, saw the nakedness of his father, and told his two brethren without. And Shem and Japheth took a garment, and laid it upon both their shoulders, and went backward, and covered the nakedness of their father; and their faces were backward, and they saw not their father's nakedness. And Noah awoke from his wine, and knew what his younger son had done unto him. And he said, Cursed be Canaan; a servant of servants shall he be unto his brethren. (Genesis Chapter 9:20-25)

The Bible speaks of Noah being a farmer, who was the first to plant a vineyard. Once he harvested the bountiful crops, he tasted the product of his hard work. Obviously he tasted too much of his wine, because as the scriptures describe, Noah gets drunk and ultimately passed out. In the meanwhile, his son Ham saw his father naked in his private tent, passed out sleeping. As a result, Ham told his two brothers, he had seen his father's nakedness exposed, so they decided to protect their father by covering his naked body. As they covered their dad, these two used wisdom and did not look at their father in this state.

As you see in this story, the results of Noah's drinking problem affected the entire family to the point of destroying Ham's lineage. There are so many negative results that are caused by engaging in too much wine, as God warns us in Ephesians Chapter 5:18 *"Do not get drunk on wine, which leads to debauchery. Instead be filled with the spirit."* Earlier in that passage, we are warned to be careful on how we live, and make wise choices.

Debauchery means having bad or immoral behavior that involves sex, drugs, alcohol, etc. (Merriam-Webster Dictionary)

Whenever people engage in too much of anything, the results are almost always excessive indulgence and immoral corruptness. Staying sober and avoiding over drinking helps to maintain a good judgement, and as a result, making good decisions. One negative judgement can change the future for everyone involved, especially your family members who are usually innocent by-standers.

Alcohol has been causing drama in family relationships since the days of Noah. Through Noah, God cursed an entire nation. From that time until now, alcoholism hurts everyone in the family, including the person addicted. Alcoholism sort of sneaks up like a hissing sound of a snake, before you see it, you can hear it's deadly sound and before you can react to the bite, the deadly and the poisonous venom has already entered the veins of the victim. Some snake bites are so deadly, paralysis is the initial result then ultimately death.

This example of the snake bite is what happens to families all over the world, but especially in the United States. The children and loved ones of alcoholics oftentimes take the brunt of the blow. Having to grow up in such a hostile environment and cope with situations often too young for a child to comprehend. The spouse of an alcoholic may often experience verbal and physical abuse. Victims of alcoholism are left battered for years to come, and the effects go deep and wide. I cannot stress enough how death can end the life of a loved one, but also destroy an entire family. Biblically speaking, every one of us has a descendant of this terrible disease in our bloodline.

LOT'S FOOLISH DAUGHTERS

*One day the older daughter said to the younger, "Our father is getting old and there's not a man left in the country by whom we can get pregnant. Let's get our father **drunk** with **wine** and lay with him. We'll get children through our father—it's our **only** chance to keep our family alive." Genesis 19:31-32*

This is another example of making unwise decisions based on drinking too much wine. These daughters were trying to help in a twisted sort of way, but obviously did not understand they were causing more harm than good. Here we see the results of Noah's vineyard, creeping into future generations that possibly did not even know him. These are the deadly effects of drinking, not only can you lose your health and life, but your choices can result in disobedience and loss of future inheritances.

Although, Lot seemed to be the victim in this scenario, we discovered later how the progeny of this sin resulted in two lines of generations that remained wicked and God damned. Don't be like these daughters who caused their own seed to be cursed. Again, alcohol ruins families for generations. Alcoholism is a disease that transfers from generation to generation, ending in tragedy until someone finally stops the cycle. Will that someone be you?

FAMILY HISTORY

Alcoholism tends to run in families genetically due to many factors. Some folks grow up drinking socially and have no issues at all, while coincidentally, others can't seem to realize when the last drink should have been several glasses ago and few hours back. No matter where you see yourself, alcoholism is a serious illness and is no respecter of race, culture, social standards or financial means. Anyone can go down into the snare set by alcohol when used unwisely and used too frequently. Alcoholism may lead to the use of prescription drugs as well as illegal recreational use. Untame the beast and it won't be long; the entire family line can be destroyed for generations.

Visit any of the thousands or even millions of men incarcerated and one common thread will be alcohol. Most of them may have been drinking before or after the crime was committed. Why is this, you ask? This is because for many people, alcohol numbs the pain that is often accompanied by having a family member who is also addicted to beer or hard liquor. And as the saying goes, where there is smoke, there is fire.

ABUSE IN CHILDHOOD

Unfortunately, many children are abused annually in multiple ways as a result of living in a home of one or more alcoholics. Abandonment, mental and physical abuse includes neglect and in worst cases death. The long term effects children often experience can be overlooked or unnoticed, but can show up in areas of homework and in severe cases. Some children tend to draw back and may be very timid. Minor kids in this type of environment may not be capable of communicating how they feel, and then paying close attention to body language is really important.

ABUSE IN ADULTHOOD

Oftentimes, men will most often be aggressive and abusive with their wives or girlfriends when they have had too much to drink. Statistics show that most domestic violence happens when alcohol or drugs are involved. According to a recent JAMA (Journal of American Medical Association) Report; 92 percent of domestic violence cases, alcohol was involved. In many instances, situations of abuse end in separation of families. In another report, 48-87 percent of batterers were under the influence at the time of the abuse or altercations.

Alone, alcohol cannot make anyone abusive, because and of course, one can abuse with no alcohol use at all. Nevertheless, God has warned us over and over in the scriptures to avoid getting drunk and over-excessive drinking because doing so can help us resist temptation of all kinds. Basically, we just think better with a clear and sober mind and we also make better judgments.

NO BOUNDARIES

Boundaries are necessary to protect us, but if crossed, we are left without protection. Oftentimes, alcoholics and those who love them can both remain in a stupor, or a state of denial. Some loved ones actually cope with the abuse, torn family dynamics in a state of co-dependency, allowing the victim to continue to cross boundaries time and time again. Some of the boundaries can turn into barriers. Abuse, neglect, poor communication, arguments and assaults, including sexual, physical and emotional abuse can be the result.

If children are involved, it is imperative to protect them at all cost, and if you know someone who is in an abusive situation, do not close your eyes and remain silent in denial, but do something or say something.

If you are in an abusive relationship, get help today.

Most times, people may not discern they are in an abusive relationship because they are used to being in one. Perhaps their father, mother, uncle or cousin was affected and now they think these abusive behaviors are all normal in their eyes. Well, it is not normal to abuse others, no matter what! Verbal language, hitting and sexual assault, are all abnormal behaviors and should not be allowed no matter who the assailant is, male or female.

If you are in an abusive relationship, how much danger are you in? Have boundaries been crossed? How do you know? Keep reading and if you can answer yes to any of the questions below, get help now from a police officer, counselor, priest, clergyman, nurse or physician. These are all first responders who are trained and will know how to help or guide you to the right direction to get help.

1. Are you constantly being hit or beaten by another adult?
2. Have you been slapped, pushed, punched, or kicked?
3. Do you have new or an old bruise, cuts, scrapes or burns at the hands of someone else?
4. Has anyone spit on you, cursed you and constantly call you out of your name? (Verbal abuse)
5. Have you been locked up in a room, closet, storage unit, garage, or attic/basement for any length of time?
6. Has anyone threatened to kill you, your children or take your life?
7. Does your boyfriend or girlfriend threaten your

family or friends if you discuss your relationship with anyone?

8. Have you been raped, or forced to have sex with anyone against your will?

9. Are you being ignored, or not being taken care of (food, shelter, and clothing) needs or neglect?

10. Has anyone pointed a weapon (gun or knife) at you and threatened you bodily harm?

The list above is not all-inclusive, but the above is intended to give you an idea of the multiple ways abuse can be caused by others. These examples are simply to help open your eyes and get help if you are affected by any one of the above signs and symptoms of abuse.

CHAOS AND CONFUSION

Homes impacted by chaos and confusion are unfortunately a common occurrence today. If you are living in chaos and confusion from day to day, just note, this is not God's doing.

*For God is not the **author of confusion, but of** peace, as in all the churches of the saints. 1 Corinthians 14:33 (NKJV)*

In the passage above, God is setting the order of His Church, but this scripture can be also prescribed to every area of our lives, especially in our family situations. God brings peace to our family if we place Him in the center. Developing a time of prayer personally and as a family will not give the devil any room to come in and destroy God's greatest investment on earth, the family.

Ellaina's Story:

My Beginnings

Our upbringing with our dad, growing up in a family with four children. My mother had mental issues and she did go to church, praying constantly asking God to heal her. My dad on the other hand was a good father, but was a womanizer. Often times my dad was not always around and was hardly home. We would constantly look for affirmations from him that seldom came. Thank God I had a Big Daddy in the sky who did affirm me. Thank God for his affirmation.

Scripture to Ponder: *Do not give place to the devil. Ephesians 4:27 (KJV)*

Conclusion: Do not give the enemy *devices* (alcoholism, addictive behaviors or abuse) a foothold, room, or an opportunity to take over your family. Protect your family at all cost by dealing with the issues as soon as you see/discern them in your loved one, yourself or your children. In any case, seek help immediately.

CHAPTER TWO

Codependency

Ye have heard that it hath been said, Thou shalt love thy neighbor, and hate thine enemy. But I say unto you. Love your enemies, bless them that curse you, do good to them that hate you; and pray for them which despitefully use you, and persecute you.

If you find yourself asking these questions, you may just be co-dependent. Later in this chapter I will share with you how to overcome co-dependency once and for all. But first, read the following statements to see if you can identify yourself here.

1. *Why do I keep attracting the same relationships?*
2. *Why am I always angry and afraid?*
3. *Am I really important to God?*
4. *Why do I continue tolerating abuse?*

5. *Do you keep shutting down?*
6. *I feel like no one listens to me.*
7. *Why do I feel so alone?*

Now, while you are self-examining yourself, I would like to share an account of a husband and wife. The husband was very wealthy, but the bible says he was very churlish and very evil.

Now, the name of the man was Nabal; and the name of his wife Abigail: and she was a woman of good understanding, and of a beautiful countenance: but the man was churlish and evil in his doings; and he was of the house of Caleb. 1 Samuel 25:3

This passage above provides a background on the situation at hand. But later in the scriptures the story gets a little clearer.

And Abigail came to Nabal; and, behold, he held a feast in his house, like the feast of a king; and Nabal's heart was merry within him, for he was very drunken: wherefore she told him nothing, less or more, until the morning light. But it came to pass in the morning, when the wine was gone out of Nabal, and his wife had told him these things, that his heart died within him, and he became as a stone. And it came to pass about ten days after, that the LORD smote Nabal, that he died. 1 Samuel 25:36-38

Please understand that I do not have room in this chapter on co-dependency to discuss the story of David, Nabal and Abigail in its entirety. But allow me to share a synopsis.

Abigail was the wife of Nabal, and several times in 1 Samuel Chapter 25, he was noted as "the son of Belial", once by his wife and another by his own servants of his own household. Who would know him any better? I'll tell you who. God knows him and his heart was hard as stone. His servants also noted something very interesting, they mentioned, "He would not listen to any man."

Co-dependency affects everyone in the household of the alcoholic or the person who just won't listen to the wisdom or Godly counsel. Their decisions affect everyone involved. In the case of Nabal, he was a terror in his own household, he was a drunkard and according to God, he was among those who "pisseth against a wall." What does this term mean? Below we will discuss this term as well as describe the "son of Belial."

The term "pisseth against the wall" is a term describing the "male" species, however, in this text makes it clear; Nabal was not going to leave any man standing, as he would kill them all. This was evil in the sight of God, and unfortunately, his wife was not happy and took matters into her own hands out of desperation. Who knows how long she had been living in these circumstances, with the "son of Belial."

In Hebrew the word, "Belial" is translated as "worthless." Now that is self-explanatory, but to dig deeper, the word also means, "yokeless" or "unyoked." In other words, Abigail was unequally yoked to this evil man who was nothing less than a drunkard and a murderer. Who knows how abusive he may have been towards her, but considering the times, she was desperate enough to almost throw herself at David to save herself from her evil husband. Later, as the text reads, her husband died and David proposed and took her as his own wife.

Wrapping up, this situation may have been a little over the top, but similar situations or worst occur in many families of alcoholics, where there is known abuse and addiction. The bible makes it clear; drunkenness ends in wickedness, period. The results can end in adultery, divorce and terrible death. Women and children are often the main victims of abuse, therefore, get help as soon as possible. Take action and protect your children at all cost.

CO-DEPENDENCY SIMPLY DEFINED

A psychological condition in which someone is in an unhappy and unhealthy relationship that involves living with and providing care for another person (such as a drug addict or an alcoholic) (Merriam-Webster Dictionary)

Now let's dive into this discussion. What are the behaviors of those suffering with co-dependency? Who are co-dependents? Why do they become co-dependent, anyway? These are very complicated questions. I wish I could answer them scientifically or physically, but I will make every attempt to answer them biblically. Again, I am not a certified counselor, psychiatrist, or a medical doctor. However, I have experienced co-dependency and co-dependent behaviors first hand, based on personal experience.

Co-dependents suffer unintentionally and often times in silence. This is a phenomenon because many times they assist the abuser or addicted loved one in the act. They may even purchase the alcohol or drugs for their family member and in worst case scenarios, encourage the behavior to keep the peace. For example, the victim has often lived in fear and searching for peace, so out of desperation, they attempt to help "keep the peace" by avoiding confrontation and never telling the alcoholic "No, I won't buy you another drink." "No, I will not take you to the liquor store."

Another word for people like this is an "enabler" needing approval or affection from this addicted individual who may be a mother, father, son, daughter, spouse or lover. Enablers often make attempts to cover for their loved one or hide behind their excuses to remain in the situation, often thinking they are doing it for "love, respect or honor." But these are just excuses. Please note, if you are an "enabler", you are not helping the person; you are only prolonging their addiction and causing more harm to the entire situation. Most importantly and indirectly, you are hurting yourself. Be stern, ask God for a spirit of boldness and tell the person you are caring for, a word that will help everyone involved and that word is "NO!"

Who are co-dependents really, down deep inside? Well, they are people like you and me who have big hearts that love to give back, especially to those we love. But, nevertheless, somewhere down deep they have been hurt. Have you ever heard the saying, "Hurt people, hurt people?" Well, this statement is as self-explanatory as it gets; people who hurt, often hurt others, whether intentionally or un-intentionally. These individuals have often remained numb to their own pain and are willing to take on even more pain, no matter how difficult life becomes for them. At the forefront of their minds, they are enduring for the love of their life.

How do co-dependents become enablers in the first place? The behavior of the enabler is very unhealthy as I stated earlier, so below I have gathered some behaviors or descriptions of these people who for no reason of their own, gives more than necessary to "save" someone else who is so close to them it hurts. The enablers motto ironically, is often "give until it hurts."

Below are 10 common personality traits found in an enabler.

1. *Low self-esteem*
2. *Fixers-believer they can "change"them*
3. *Broken emotionally*
4. *Addictive personalities*
5. *Depressed, Suppressed or Oppressed*
6. *Emotionally Dependent*
7. *Weak-easily controlled by others*
8. *Empty, need a void filled*
9. *Loneliness*
10. *Dependent on others*

The areas above are common among most co-dependents and some of their addicted loved ones. Knowing the signs to look for can help solve the problems that may result and grow increasingly worse as time goes on. Bottom line, these toxic behaviors and personality traits are not from God; they are from the evil one and should be dealt with spiritually as well as medically as deemed necessary.

As Christians, we are commanded to, ***"Be sober, be vigilant; because your adversary the devil, as a roaring lion, walketh about, seeking whom he may devour."*** 1 Peter 5:8

This word "sober" is the opposite of being "drunken" and in addition we are to remain sober at all times. "Sober" means, "not addicted to intoxicating drinks" or "not drunk." In addition, it means "sober minded." In other words, keep your "MIND" sober. Dependency is the ultimate reward for any person, but co-dependency is like being a slave in chains, leaving one person chained to another person both physically and spiritually immobile, stuck, unable to move forward likened to being in quicksand. Another way of looking at dependency is likened to a "spirit of heaviness," with no one around to lift the heaven burden and unbearable yoke of bondage. But there is good news; Jesus' is our burden bearer and our burden lifter. Jesus anointing destroys all yokes!

And it shall come to pass in that day, that his burden shall be taken away from off thy shoulder, and his yoke from off thy neck and the yoke shall be destroyed because of the anointing. Romans 8:37 (KJV)

Ellaina's Story:

The Wrecking Ball of Abuse

On one day, I will never forget, my Dad loaded a shotgun that had 6 bullets in it. Also, on the table there were 6 shot glasses lined up, and his plan was to shoot all of us, one shot glass for each of us. He would take a drink for each of us, my Mom, my siblings and me. Then his plan was to ultimately take his own life as well. A knock on the door from my older brother, praise God, stopped our would be fate of killing our entire family. At the time, I was only ten years old, but I was old enough to understand something terribly bad could have happened that day. Praise God we were spared.

Scriptures to Ponder: *"It is not for kings, O Lemuel--not for kings to drink wine, not for rulers to crave beer, lest they drink and forget what the law decrees, and deprive all the oppressed of their rights. Give beer to those who are perishing, wine to those who are in anguish; let them drink and forget their poverty and remember their misery no more." Proverbs 31:4-7 (NIV)*

Conclusion: Be aware, co-dependency can be a mental or spiritual illness and affects everyone involved. Marriages and the family unit are important to God and should be protected. The enemy devices will never win and cannot win against the marriage God has put together. If you find your marriage threatened and can't seem to find the strength to fight the enemy on your own; find a good, Bible teaching church, read God's word often and ask prayer warriors to surround you in prayer, getting into an agreement for your success. Lastly, get professional help from a medical doctor and do not hesitate to ask for help. If you are suicidal, call 911 and let the professionals take care of you properly until your own Faith is built up and you are strong again.

Nay, in all these things we are more than conquerors through him that loved us. Romans 8:37 (KJV)

God makes us free! Walk in your place of liberty today!

Stand fast therefore in the liberty wherewith Christ hath made us free, and be not entangled again with the yoke of bondage. Behold, I Paul say unto you, that if ye be circumcised, Christ shall profit you nothing. For I testify again to every man that is circumcised, that he is a debtor to do the whole law. Christ is become of no effect unto you, whosoever of you are justified by the law; ye are fallen from grace. For we through the Spirit wait for the hope of righteousness by faith. For in Jesus Christ neither circumcision availeth anything, nor uncircumcision; but faith which worketh by love. Ye did run well; who did hinder you that ye should not obey the truth? This persuasion cometh not of him that calleth you. A little leaven leaveneth the whole lump. Galatians 5:1-9 (KJV)

CHAPTER THREE

Emotional Soul Ties

Dear friends, I urge you, as foreigners and ex-
iles, to abstain from sinful desires, which wage
war against your soul. 1 Peter 2:11 (KJV)
And the very God of peace sanctify you whol-
ly; and I pray God your whole spirit and
soul and body be preserved blameless unto
the coming of our Lord Jesus Christ. 1 Thes-
salonians 5:23 (KJV)

Abuse and bitterness are the ugly side-effects of a family deeply drowning in the disease of alcoholism.

In this chapter, I would like to go a little deeper into the spiritual side of how alcoholism starts in the first place within the victim of the spiritually oppressed.

There are spiritual "open-doors" that allow the enemy to creep in through generations of people in families from all nationalities, social cultural differences and financial economic diversities. Finding the common denomination is not difficult as we look from the lenses of a spiritual or biblical perspective, we can quickly find the culprit. His name is Satan and he is a deceiver, a liar and the Father of lies.

Below are a few scriptures that confirm my position. Again, I give you a disclaimer. I am not a professional counselor, medical doctor or psychiatrist; nor am I a bible scholar or certified teacher of the Bible. Again, I come from a place of experience, dealing with alcoholism and the effects of its addiction on a personal level. Alcoholism, from a spiritual perspective intricately, emotionally and physically attached itself to those I love and slithered into my family causing spiritual havoc and even resulted in physical death.

I have lost some who were very close to me and from that perspective, I feel I am a credible witness to share my insight book with you.

Professionally speaking, I have an honorary experience "PhD" in traumatic experiences, toxic relationships and abuse. Therefore, God has assigned this burden on me to assist others to escape the trenches of this disease and get help immediately, according to your faith. God is able to heal anyone of this ailment, but first you need information and next you need to believe He can and He will.

The spirit of the Lord GOD is upon me; because the LORD has anointed me to preach good tidings unto the meek; he has sent me to bind up the brokenhearted, to proclaim liberty to the captives, and the opening of the prison to them that are bound. Isaiah 61:1 (KJV)

In 2 Corinthians, the bible speaks of spiritual weapons. For though we live in the world, we do not wage war as the world does. The weapons we fight with are not the weapons of the world. On the contrary, they have divine power to demolish strongholds. We demolish arguments and every pretension that sets itself up against the knowledge of God, and we take captive every thought to make it obedient to Christ. 2 Corinthians 10:3-5 (KJV)

In other words, we do not fight with guns and knives or stones; therefore, we must fight against spiritual weapons. Doesn't it make perfect sense, if our foe, our enemy is fighting us with a spiritual arsenal, we must in turn fight back spiritually. Now, this passage places these in categories: arguments, pretensions, strongholds and thoughts. All of these are mind traps or word traps. Therefore, this passage makes it clear; our fight is a battle in our minds. All spiritual wars are fought in the mind. God has given us a remedy or weaponry to fight back… we fight the enemy with faith filled words, based on God's word found in the Bible. This is the only way to win the battle, with our mouth.

Have you ever noticed or thought about how addiction really starts? That's a very simple answer, but I will give it to you straight. All addictive behaviors begin in the MIND and end in the MOUTH.

For as he thinketh in his heart, so is he: Eat and drink, saith he to thee; but his heart is not with thee. Proverbs 23:7 (KJV)

Since you have purified your souls by obedience to the truth, so that you have a genuine love for your brothers, love one another deeply, from a pure heart. 1 Peter 1:22 (KJV)

This word "heart" goes beyond the physical organ beating in your chest. The heart is the soul of man or the mind of man, meaning our intellect, will and emotions.

Basically, the heart of man is what God searches to find how he or she is really thinking. Now our minds are very intricate and include both a conscience and a sub-conscience. Now, I will not bore you with the science behind a man's inner man (the spirit and soul) but I can tell you the enemy devices are always aimed at the MIND of Man. For this reason, a man/woman should always be guarding our minds. God knew this very well, so he gave us some armor to wear at all times in order to stand against the "wiles" (Mind Trap) of the enemy.

"Put on the full armor of God so that you can take your stand against the devil's schemes. For our struggle is not against flesh and blood, but against the rulers, against the authorities, against the powers of this dark world and against the spiritual forces of evil in the heavenly realms." Ephesians 6: 10-18 (KJV)

Below is a list of "Mind Traps" I created. Many alcoholics, caregivers, enablers and other addictive personalities (strongholds, arguments, pretensions and thoughts) often fall into traps like these.

1. *Twisted Love*
2. *Self-hate*
3. *Bitterness*
4. *Battered*
5. *Toxic Relationships*
6. *Lies*
7. *Bitterroots*
8. *Unforgiving*
9. *Anger*
10. *Hatred*

Remember love covers a multitude of sins. Therefore first... love yourself, and then you can love others unconditionally as Jesus loves us.

And above all things have fervent charity among yourselves: for charity shall cover the multitude of sins. 1 Peter 4:8 (KJ V)

So, now that we have learnt the spiritual devices of the enemy, let's look closer at soul ties. To be "tied" together in the soulish (MIND) areas is not good, God forbids this.

Regarding marriage, *God says the husband will leave his mother and father and cleave to his wife, and they will become "one flesh"* according to Genesis 2:24, but not "one soul." There is a difference. The soulish areas are likened to the will, emotions and feelings of man; remember this can be dangerous places or strongholds of the enemy to set up spiritual offenses or dangerous "mind traps." Remember our weapon is in our mouth... the word of God. But before we get the word in our mouths, we must get it in our hearts, or it will not work for us. Remember the heart has several chambers and there is a flow of activity or "blood" going in and out. If we miss this teaching, please read this chapter again before moving forward.

Soul ties are not acceptable, and should be cut immediately. Soul ties are simply strongholds or assaults of the enemy of the mind. The best way to deal with these strongholds is to pull them down. Don't allow the enemy to play mind games and make you fall into the mind trap. Remember our weapons are mighty through our God! Pull those strongholds in your mind down with the word of God. When the enemy lies to you, talk back over and over with the word of God until he can no longer entrap you in the tangled web of deception and lies. You do not have to stay where you are, there is help for ungodly alliances, unfruitful relationships and yes, even soul ties; and His name *is Jesus. Say this with me, "I will lift up mine eyes unto the hills, from whence cometh my help. My help comes from the LORD, who made heaven and earth." (A Song of degrees.) Psalms 121:1-2 (KJV)*

Ellaina's Story:

Their System Versus His System

(My opinion) The court system does not care about the kids. It seems no one looks out for the kids. In many cases, lawyers who are greedy, often leave the families they are supposed to help stay broken, leaving scattered pieces to pick up. My family dynamics were very rough and my mother held it all together in the strength I know only God could have given her. The System wasn't there for us, but God was definitely with us.

Scripture to Ponder: *Love is patient, love is kind. It does not envy, it does not boast, it is not proud. 1 Corinthians 13:4 (KJV)*

Conclusion:

Soul Ties are Real!

Remember, don't confuse close relationships like girl/boyfriend and mother/father, sisters and brothers as soul-ties. This is an error; soul ties occur usually when a person gets so entangled and intertwined in an ungodly type of relationship. They lose their self-identity, neglect their own needs and/or imitate the behavior of another individual. Lastly, soul ties may occur when someone totally misrepresents or confuses a relationship from a one-sided point of view.

Again, these assaults take place in the minds and when offenses occur, this is a sure signal that your mind has been taken over by the assault of the enemy. I wish I had time to go deeper into spiritual warfare and the tricks of the enemy. Stay tuned, more books on these subjects are coming soon.

Don't stop here, keep reading. Chapter 4 will definitely expound on what we have just covered. Don't give up, you are almost free. Your shackles have been loosened and liberty is yours, today!

CHAPTER FOUR

Manipulation

Watch out for false prophets. They come to you in sheep's clothing, but inwardly they are ferocious wolves. By their fruit you will recognize them. Matthew 7:15-16

IS IT YOU OR IS IT EVERYONE ELSE?

Manipulation is a demonic spirit that often masks itself and hides in fear, anger, anxiety or depression. The act of one human being attempting to control and exploit another human being stems from a spirit of control and is usually harnessed by aggression and lies. Alcoholics often allow dysfunction to control them, because they are rooted in the false realization of the truth. Living with family members who are alcoholics are coming from an environment surrounded by inconsistency and irrational behaviors, most likely you have encountered a spirit named Jezebel.

Now in the book of Esther, there was a Queen named Vashti, who had to deal with a drunken King named Xerxes. After drinking to stupor, he became angry with his wife because she refused to be embarrassed publicly by his charades. The Biblical account in Esther Chapter 1 goes like this:

By the king's command each guest was allowed to drink with no restrictions, for the king instructed all the wine stewards to serve each man what he wished. Queen Vashti also gave a banquet for the women in the royal palace of King Xerxes. On the seventh day, when King Xerxes was in high spirits from wine, he commanded the seven eunuchs who served him—Mehuman, Biztha, Harbona, Bigtha, Abagtha, Zethar and Karkas—to bring before him Queen Vashti, wearing her royal crown, in order to display her beauty to the people and nobles, for she was lovely to look at. But when the attendants delivered the king's command, Queen Vashti refused to come. Then the king became furious and burned with anger. Esther 1:8-12 (KJV)

Basically, Queen Vashti refused to be abused by her husband and stood up for herself. The Bible does not say how often this occurred, but if I could imagine, this possibly wasn't the first time and at this point she was probably furious. Now King Xerxes had reigned approximately three years at this time and it was custom for the King to summon his bride at least once per year. So let's just say, he acted in this manner at least twice before. Well, as far as she was concerned, twice was too much and thrice would have been more than she could take. Let's read on to see what the King did next in his drunkenness.

After the King sought wisdom from his counsel, this was the result as noted in the following passage of scripture:

"According to law, what must be done to Queen Vashti?"
he asked. "She has not obeyed the command of King Xerxes
that the eunuchs have taken to her."

Then Memukan replied in the presence of the king and the
nobles, "Queen Vashti has done wrong, not only against the
king, but also against all the nobles and the peoples of all the
provinces of King Xerxes. For the queen's conduct will become
known to all the women, and so they will despise their husbands
and say, 'King Xerxes commanded Queen Vashti to be brought
before him, but she would not come.' This very day the Persian
and Median women of the nobility who have heard about the
queen's conduct will respond to all the king's nobles in the same
way. There will be no end of disrespect and discord.

"Therefore, if it pleases the king, let him issue a royal
decree, and let it be written in the laws of Persia and Media,
which cannot be repealed, that Vashti is never again to enter
the presence of King Xerxes. Also, let the king give her royal
position to someone else who is better than she. Then when
the king's edict is proclaimed throughout all his vast realm,
all the women will respect their husbands, from the least to
the greatest." Esther 1:15-20 (KJV)

According to the law of the land, King Xerxes was
forced to oust his wife, without hesitation. His decision in
his drunkenness was unwise, but the damage was done, and
now the women in the province would now see how they
would be treated as well if, like Queen Vashti, they refused
to follow the orders of their husband. I have one word for
this type of decision making, MANIPULATION.

There are women in abusive relationships similar to that
described in the above text. Women all over the world are
subject to the laws of man, instead of the laws of God. Some-

one's pleasure often becomes someone else's pain and vice versa. I am so glad Queen Vashti took a stand and no matter how you interpret this scripture, whether it be culture of the day, the times, or even sexism, manipulation caused an entire kingdom's female citizen population to hurt at another woman's expense. Now I do understand the brevity of the story of Esther. How she was a brave young virgin who saved an entire People (The Israelites) by preparing to take Vashti's place and marry the King. However, I am coming from the perspective of the effects of alcoholism and abuse, so excuse me for a moment, so we can concentrate on the matter at hand; a hurting woman at the hands of an addictive personality ends up homeless and abandoned.

This could be the headline of many newspapers across the country, but you won't see that any time soon, because most people think of alcoholism as the family secret that won't' disappear, but is kept shoved under the rug.

Merriam-Webster dictionary defines "Manipulation" as *to control or play upon by artful, unfair, or insidious means especially to one's own advantage.*

However, on the other hand the meaning can be looked at physically as well, actually "moving an object in one's hands to treat or in a skillful manner."

As the king, Xerxes had every right to do what he did, but it doesn't make his decision a fair one. Manipulation can be negative or positive, but in this teaching, we will look at it as the art of the devil's playground, to be avoided at all cost. Below is what the Bible says about manipulation.

David said to him, "If you pass over with me, then you will be a burden to me. "But if you return to the city, and say to Absalom,'I will be your servant, O king; as I have been

your father's servant in time past, so I will now be your ser-
vant,' then you can thwart the counsel of Ahithophel for me.

In the above passage, David used the word "thwart"
meaning, to prevent (someone) from doing something or to
stop (something) from happening; now again in either case
the word can be negative or positive, depending on whose
side you are on. Now personally, if your manipulation of a
situation brings harm to another person, then it is wrong.

Manipulative people are often operating in witchcraft,
which is rebellion and should understand getting people to
do things that are against their personal will is manipulation.

Alcoholics and other addictive personalities often manipulate the people closest to them, or in some cases, people who don't know them well in order to get what they desire, which is usually a quick fix until the next opportunity
to manipulate that person again strikes. This behavior can
be harmful and hurtful, often leaving invisible scars that
last for years. Caregivers can be enablers, but they should
not be manipulated for any reason. Manipulation is abuse.
Below are some ways those dealing with addictions manipulate their family and those who love them.

**The manipulator or mind controller often demon-
strates unproductive behaviors such as:**
1. *Lack of respect for the victim.*
2. *Uses threats and fear tactics to control their victim.*
3. *Often uses criticism or harsh language when talking
   to the victim.*
4. *Always yells and bark orders at the victim.*
5. *Uses social isolation, keep the victim from family and
   friends.*

6. *Attacks the victim's knowledge and perception of various subjects.*
7. *Keeps information under wraps.*

These seven observations are not at all inclusive and there could be tons more, but for the sake of time, I want you to see some common areas where manipulators can be aggressive, with the end result being controlling another person's soul. Don't allow the enemy's influence of another person control your life. Break free today. Remember, on the other side of doubt is faith, and as your faith grows you get stronger and stronger knowing God is with you always!

Ellaina's Story:

My Baby Sister

My sister died young. She went through so many issues that most were either covered up or overlooked. She was such a sweet spirited, outgoing person who would do a lot for you, but she was so kind and was often misused because of it. She never learned to stand up for herself unless of course someone was beating her up in the park. She had the face of an angel, loving God with her whole heart with worldly taste when it came to things. Her shopping habits often got the best of her, but I think she wasn't strong enough to fight the demons she dealt with.

Scripture to Ponder: *"Be strong and courageous, do not be afraid or tremble at them, for the LORD your God is the one who goes with you. He will not fail you or forsake you. "Deuteronomy 31:6 (KJV)*

Conclusion:

Control is Manipulation!

Manipulation is rooted in a controlling spirit. Again, the enemy set up strongholds in your mind, and as they are rehearsed mentally, the victim begins to believe the lies of Satan as the truth. Mind control is a weapon and can be distinguished on contact with the truth, the Word of God. Manipulation is also abuse. Again, find help and get out of danger. If you are in a dangerous situation, there is an escape route. Jesus is that escape route in the spiritual, but in the physical, just get up from where you are and go. If you find yourself under any type of control, (mental abuse/spiritual abuse) in many ways is just as dangerous or may be more dangerous than physical abuse. Remember the enemy may try to assault you, but no weapon in his arsenal can harm you.

Say this with me, "No *weapon forged against me, shall prosper and any tongue that rises up against me, I shall condemn." Isaiah 54:17 (KJV)*

That word, "forged" means formed, and better explained, this scripture means my faith filled words will also form a hedge of protection or a shield around me and the fiery darts of the enemy cannot penetrate my mind, will, intellect, emotions or my heart. As my mouth speaks the Word of God, this is my greatest weapon against the plans of the enemy.

CHAPTER FIVE

The Revolving Door

"Dear friends, do not believe every spirit, but test the spirits to see whether they are from God, because many false prophets have gone out into the world. 1 John 4:1

Enablers are people who commonly make every attempt or excuse to placate, negotiate or protect the negative actions of those they love or love them. However, FreeDictionary. com defines enablers as a person who encourages or enables negative or self-destructive behavior in another or a person or thing that makes something possible. Obviously, this can be rational to individuals, both positive and negative, but for the objective of this book I am reviewing the negative results that are caused by enablers and the ones who love them.

Woe unto him that gives his neighbor drink that presses your wineskin to him, and makes him drunk also, that you may look on his nakedness! Habakuk 2:15

This text describes an individual who actually provides the alcohol, purchases it, brings it home and pours and pours for the addicted person until they are drunk to stupor to make any logical decisions and no longer have a sound mind. Actually, it is impossible for them too. When our mind is not clear, our conscience is left unprotected and we are no longer able to make decisions for ourselves, from simple to complex, which could be life changing.

Enablers are usually people who try to overcompensate for a loved one who is addicted. They are the ones who usually suffer silently with the ability to act, as well as look the part of a fixer. As a fixer, they cope with the abuse in spite of the pain. Enablers are never separated from the pain experience, they simply tolerate until the worst occurs, and they give up and break down until it is too late to recognize that nothing they have done has ever helped their loved one in the first place.

There are five lessons or eye openers to be assessed or learned from the enabler, as I have listed them below. Please approach these lessons as examples only, because every situation is different. Husbands, wives, their children, sisters and brothers can all be identified as enablers as well as victims. Remember, it is only until the enabler can see themselves as a victim or martyr, only then will the healing truly begin.

The Characteristics of an Enabler

Enablers always struggle with the following questions. ***Should I Stay or Should I Go?*** The decision to leave or remain in a place of abuse in any form is difficult for anyone to answer because there are often so many variables. Perhaps there are children involved, the spouse can't afford to support themselves or another reason may be the victim is just so tied up into the situation emotionally, they can't see themselves anywhere else. No matter what, there is always a way of escape, God sees to our landing in a safe place.

What Am I Really Getting Out of This? Now, this question seems to go in the opposite direction of all of the other points discussed thus far. Even after multiple embarrassing moments that have been unforgivable as it seems. Many of us wonder how we are going to get past the hurt, the pain and yes the unforgettable embarrassment that goes on behind closed doors in many homes of alcoholics. You can name your own experience below along with the price you have had to pay to get past the pain.

Below there are *three blanks left empty* in order for you to fill in because oftentimes we have to write words down concerning us, because sometimes the accrual of these situations cause us to suppress the pain continually, along with the problems that come along for the ride.

Answer this question in 3 words. **Why can't I put myself first?**

a. _____

b. _____

c. _____

What Is the Acceptance of My Reality? *Many enablers find it so difficult to manage this very honest question regarding their own* **REALITY.**

Reality *is defined as "the world or the state of things as they actually exist, as opposed to an idealistic or notional idea of them."*

Listen, do you really know if you are living in the "experience" of how you wished life was versus how life really is? This means, do you really know who you are, where you are, and who you are really living with?

Face the TRUTH! Are you living in a toxic environment? Remember the children are living in this situation too!

Remember codependents feed inside of environments of insanity just like the bottom feeders chomp away down deep in the dark bottom of the ocean. Often filling themselves with the toxicity of the environment they live in. As a result, children involved are also deeply infected and seem invisible because they internalize their pain. Children are often taught to be "seen and not heard" so their symptoms often manifest in abdominal pain, headaches and loss of appetite.

Common occurrences of the police being called to these residences are not rare and this leaves children wondering if their parents will ever live in harmony, especially if an arrest is issued. Once the police are involved, decisions must be made to remain in such an unhealthy relationship. Don't do it for the kids, because the children deserve so much more. There comes a time when the sober parent needs to make a "sober minded" judgement call once the fog lifts for the best interest of the children, including the entire family, even the alcoholic.

Your children see your fighting and if they don't see it, they definitely can feel the tension in the home. Stop trying to hide. Your neighbors may not say anything, but your children may be telling them what is going on inside your home, believe this or not! Neighbors do gossip and whisper behind your back. Your family and friends are talking as well. Even church members may know about your situation and nothing is done. Enablers choose to live in this sort of hell anyway, ignoring the signs of their own children, and loved ones who are screaming silently for help. Please stop now and breath, in and out, let your mind think; make clear choices for yourself and your loved ones, especially your children.

Or, are you simply pretending things are the way you imagine or are they the way they really are? **These are important questions to ask yourself because of the following:**

1. *Are there any hidden agendas?*
2. *I Don't Like to Be Alone*
3. *Am I a People Pleaser?*
4. *I am often nervous in social settings. (Social anxiety)*
5. *Post-Traumatic Stress Disorder*

Understand the difference between "helping and enabling" your loved one.

These are just a few statements enablers often say to themselves, making excuses for them to continue to enable those they love.

1. *"I am only trying to help them."*
2. *"They are such a good person."*
3. *"It really doesn't bother me."*
4. *"I love being available for them."*
5. *"They are my 'assignment'."*

Over and over again we say the above statements in our attempt to make excuses to cover and conceal the disease of alcohol and the infirmity of abuse. However, the boundaries we set today can save them from a lifetime of pain. Pain points exhibit in many ways, sometimes there are certain events or people, alcoholics and their codependents should avoid altogether. Certain events like weddings, funerals, and birthdays can bring on a sense of dread, simply because alcohol may be served or memories of drunken stupors or embarrassing conflicts are often reminders that the problem seems it may never go away. Fear of panic attacks or setbacks cause many who deal with this disease to just stay at home and avoid conflict altogether. This can be a problem, especially when loved ones prefer to see those who have been missed over time. Learn how to set boundaries, get past the pain, and seek help. There is help available. Seek out counselors who are experienced and caring. Many times an objective listening ear can really help jumping over the embarrassing hurdles of past mistakes.

Get past the denial stage, be a part of the solution and not a part of the problem. In other words, snap out of the brain fog of life and forge into a location of having clarity and thinking through all of the stages of how you arrived from that place of chaos and begin to focus on your future. Enablers allow the revolving doors, because there are too many of them, there is safety in familiar surroundings, familiar people and familiar circumstances.

Chaos, Crisis and Drama

Chaos, Crisis and Drama are states of mind that many

enablers allow them to remain in, in spite of the pain and shame that comes with this atmospheric pressure cooker. Listen to me, these situations are not of God and are not conditioned for the normal life of a Believer.

Despite what many see on Reality TV Shows, these scenes that play out are not REALITY. These shows promote violence, advertisement for alcoholic beverage companies in order to pad their pockets while wreaking havoc on society and destroying families. Life is REAL, not REALITY. Wake up and pray, READ your Bible daily and walk in LOVE.

The Power of Love and Forgiveness

Above all, love each other deeply, because love covers over a multitude of sins. 1 Peter 4:8 (NIV)

This word love in this verse can be explained as having "intense love" love that covers, love that protects, and love that places others before yourself. This is the love Jesus had for all of us, when he died for us. His love poured out on our behalf...***His love covered and washed away all of our sins.***

Not only did His love cover and wash away our sins, His love pushed away and deleted our sins forever. You see chaos in the home, trauma in the home and a life bombarded by crisis after crisis is a life centered in sin and God is not allowed to be in the center. I write these words with boldness because God cannot be anywhere sin is.

He is a God of order, not a god of confusion. He is a God of love; his very essence is love, never hate, never chaos or crisis.

Ellaina's Story:

A Strong Mother

My dad would leave my mom with us alone for weeks at at time. He did leave some money, but most times it was not enough to go around for all of us kids. He came and went out of our lives as he pleased. The fact that we lived through those days, beatings and such. If my Dad was not beating my mom, he beat my brothers. As I watch my brother today, he is such an amazing business man. I know that God was always with us during these scary times, I feel like we are definitely miracles.

Scriptures to Ponder:

In fact, the law requires that nearly everything be cleansed with blood and without the shedding of blood there is no forgiveness. Hebrews 9:22 (NIV)

"Therefore, my friends, I want you to know that through Jesus the forgiveness of sins is proclaimed to you." Acts 13:38 (NIV)

Peter replied, "Repent and be baptized, every one of you, in the name of Jesus Christ for the forgiveness of your sins. And you receive the gift of the Holy Spirit. Acts 2:38

Conclusion:

Forgiveness Unbound!

Repentance means to turn "about face" away from your current situation and never return that way again. In doing so, you will be taking a stand against the revolving door of enablement. However, forgiveness of yourself has to come first, because if you fail to forgive yourself, you will never be able to accept forgiveness from God or from those who you have held back.

Let me explain, being an enabler "holds back" the ones you love and keeps them from getting the help they need in the first place. This is the main reason I titled this chapter, "The Revolving Door". Please note, by enabling those you care about, you are perpetuating the symptoms, the chaos, the pain of keeping the addict in chains of the disease of alcoholism. Walk away today and allow the addict to get the help they need. When I say walk away, I am not saying, "physically" walk away. But what I am telling you to do is mentally walk away from the bondage of a 'spiritual' invisible net you are caught in, like prey. Get free! Repent, Forgive and then Walk Away! Lastly, walk away in LOVE!

CHAPTER SIX

Negativity

There hath no temptation taken you but what is common to man: but God is faithful, who will not suffer you to be tempted above that ye are able; but will with the temptation also make a way to escape, that ye may be able to bear it. 1 Corinthians 10:13

Negativity breeds discontentment!

Family drama and dysfunction isn't normal for our lives. In this chapter I want to expound on how constant negativity causes toxic waste attraction. Yes, that's what I said, "toxic waste attraction" is the ability to attract toxic relationships in one's life, simply because you have allowed the drama join itself to you far too long.

Alcoholics thrive on drama and dysfunction and so do the enablers who care for them and are the closest to them. Many alcoholics are often negative and because of their illness, seldom keep promises. Alcoholics who remain in denial are even worse at keeping their promise regarding staying sober as well as honestly seeking medical help or counseling. In many cases, they may mean well, but the addiction has a choke hold on them and they find it difficult to break free.

Alcoholics in Recovery Mode

Although the recovery period can be rough, especially to the family members who live in the home and can be considerably worst for the enabler. I must stress here, this time and period can seem extremely long, but staying focused on the outcome is the key. The mood swings are the worst part, alcohol can change the personality of the addict, but during the recovery especially, the personality changes can keep the entire family on edge, always fighting and blaming one another.

Alcohol leads to brokenness and there are no mistaking changes in behavior, personality shifts, depression, nasty attitudes, and somberness and in some cases, suicidal thoughts and disorientation. Periods of withdrawals can be a very difficult experience for all, but the best option in all cases is to remain level headed and avoid negativity.

Caregivers and family members should make every effort to remain patient, caring, understanding, and supportive during this time. Otherwise, adding fuel to the fire of negativity and toxicity will only prolong the process of recovery and build a wedge or a wall up between the entire support system.

In the book of Proverbs, the Bible warns us time and again about drunkenness. Why is this? I believe God wanted us to know about the negative ramifications of becoming "drunk" or impaired by drinking in excess of what our bodies need or can handle at one sitting. Over indulging of "strong drink" changes behavior, personalities and is unbecoming.

Let's review some scriptures below:

Wine is a mocker, strong drink a brawler, and whoever is led astray by it is not wise. Proverbs 20:1 ESV

And do not get drunk with wine, for that is debauchery, but be filled with the Spirit. Ephesians 5:18 ESV

Negativity, personality flaws and arguments often accompany overuse of alcohol as noted below:

Who has a woe? Who has sorrow? Who has strife? Who has a complaint? Who has wounds without cause? Who has redness of eyes? Those who tarry long over wine; those who go to try mixed wine. Do not look at wine when it is red, when it sparkles in the cup and goes down smoothly. In the end it bites like a serpent and stings like an adder. Your eyes will see strange things, and your heart utter perverse things... Proverbs 23: 29-35 ESV

Facing Shame and Guilt

In the above scriptures, we are warned about the "long-term" effects of drinking too much wine or strong drink over a lengthy period as well as the short term issues that come with drinking. The main problem is attracting negative toxic consequences personally and relationally.

A negative personality that comes along with too much drinking, this leads to bad relationship attraction.

Remember: Bad Company corrupts good character.

Private shame is one thing, but public shame causes much heartache. Alcoholics and their drama can and will leak outside of the household, into the workplace, into social scenes and in front of the guest during family functions.

Unfortunately, children get caught in the middle between both parents; husbands and wives grow tired of covering for one another, and the worst case scenario; the police get involved having to calm down domestic violence situations.

Whenever police are called to the scene, this may result in incarceration due to public intoxication and disturbing the peace as well as violence and mayhem involving family members, neighbors or even friends of the family. The main point here is my attempt to magnify the negative responses that could happen in the lives of those who simply refuse to get help along with those who are in their support circles. One negative issue upon the heels of others is not going to make the situation better, but often results in the exact opposite. Get help before it is too late; most of all prayer always work; so pray often, pray as a family and pray with and for your support systems.

Pray the scripture based prayers/faith confessions below; use them as a guide until you see negative emotions, drama and toxic relationships disappear.

- *Jesus is my healer and He heals all of my diseases. (Exodus 15:26)*
- *The Lord will heal me, when I cry out to Him. (Psalm 30:2)*

- *The Lord forgives all my sins, and He heals all my diseases. (Psalm 103:3)*
- *I attend to God's words and they are life to me. They are health and healing to all my flesh. (Proverbs 4:20-22)*
- *The Lord will perfect that which concerns me, even the health of my mind and body. (Psalm 138:8) Source: (jmfarro.com)*

AM I WORTHY?

The *feeling* of being worthy has been just that, a feeling. Being regarded as worthy must come from within. Feelings may come and go, but the truth always prevails. Find your truth and then you can discover the answer is yes, you are worthy. Those who are co-dependent or addicted can often experience a roller coaster ride of emotions. One day, feeling up and the very next hour you can feel down in the dumps.

Feeling worthy, meaning "worth it" is also an emotion that can change from minute to minute, hour to hour and day to day.

Worth defined: the value equivalent to that of someone or something under consideration; the level at which someone or something deserves to be valued or rated.

Now ask yourself the following questions:

- *Who determines my worthiness?*
- *Am I of value to anyone, even God?*
- *How much should I be rated?*
- *How much higher should I rate myself?*
- *How do I deserve to be treated based on my worth?*

Honestly, these questions can sound kind of foolish to some, but to those who have to live and care for an addicted person, the answers to these questions can mean life or death. The enabler seems to live a lonely life, feeling they are all alone in the world. Now go back and ask yourself the above questions again, but this time remove the negativity from your situation and look on the bright side. Remember, there is always a positive way to look at your circumstances, instead of feeling unworthy or worthless; keep on reading.

Worthiness is defined clearly in **Revelation Chapter 5,** found in verse 9 demonstrates clearly the position of those who are in the family of Believers.

And they sang a new song, saying:
"You are worthy to take the scroll,
And open its seals;
For you were slain,
And have redeemed us to God by Your blood
Out of every tribe and tongue
and people and nation,
And have made us kings and
priest to our God;
And we shall reign on the earth."
Verse 12 goes on to illustrate:
…saying with a loud voice:
"Worthy is the Lamb who was slain
To receive power and riches
and wisdom,
And strength and honor and
glory and blessing!"

Let me explain, our worthiness is only found in Jesus, because He is worthy, therefore because we are in Him, we are made worthy. Apart from Him we may "feel" unworthy, but we cannot depend on our feelings after discovering the truth found in the above scriptures; our worthiness is from Him and by Him, not apart from Him.

Addiction to alcohol and all of the symptoms cause the feelings of *unworthiness*. Negative feelings often cause emotional turmoil in the lives of those living with this disease. Feelings of disappointment and despair can surmount in the hearts of loved ones who begin to lose hope that recovery will ever be successful. These feelings result in a merry-go-round of emotions and are the basis for more dysfunctional family drama to mount. Believe it or not, a strong family will survive through these negative situations if everyone remains strong and hold fast to the Worthy Lamb!

Coping Skills-Skills you need to make it through your test.

These are skills that are necessary for mental health. Below are a few that discusses what are common with those who struggle with addiction and the caregivers who love them. You are not alone; your struggle is not yours alone. Remember others are going through much of what you have to cope with as well. Always be prepared to deal with what life may throw your way.

The Why Me Syndrome-Why my kindness is taken for granted?

If you are like most people, at some point in your life you have asked the question, "Why Me, Lord?" Honestly, we all have asked God what have I ever done to end up here? Or perhaps you have asked, "How did I end up here?" If this is where you are, and you are asking God this question, then you are in the right place at the right time. Reading this page, right now, was not a coincidence. God knew you would end up where you are. He has never left you alone. Even if you "feel" lonely in your situation, this is right where God wants you to be. This question, "Why Me, Lord?" is usually asked at the point of exasperation. Once you have tried to fix all of the negativity on your own, and you can't see your way out. Perhaps like many others going through similar challenges, you have found no help, no support, and you may even realize many of the mistakes were made by you.

STOP THE BLAME GAME!

What is the blame game? The blame game starts and ends with you. This game began a long time ago in the Garden of Eden. In Genesis, after God had created the first family he placed them in the garden, and gave them explicit instructions not to eat fruit from one single tree, and reminding both of them, they could eat from any other tree, but that particular tree they were to avoid because if they ate from it, they would surely die.

Well, along came a serpent and talked the woman into tasting the fruit, just one single piece of fruit wouldn't hurt, right? Well, it did hurt, it stopped the carefree lifestyle they both had, it caused them to have to work, it exposed their sin, and nakedness and it caused all mankind to fall. Yes, all of that after eating one piece of fruit. But that wasn't the end of it, because the man refused to take responsibility, their problems had only just begun!

You may read the entire account in *Genesis Chapter 3:1-24,* but for the sake of time please read a portion of the story below.

Then the Lord God called to Adam and said to him, "Where are you?"

So he said, "I heard your voice in the garden, and I was afraid because I was naked; and I hid myself."

And He said, "Who told you that you were naked? Have you eaten from the tree of which I commanded you that you should not eat?"

Then the man said, "The woman who you gave to be with me, she gave me of the tree and I ate."

And the Lord God said to the woman, "What is this you have done?"

The woman said, "The serpent deceived me, and I ate." Genesis 3: 9-13

Can you see the "blame game" throughout that passage; the serpent tricked the woman, the woman blamed the serpent and the man blamed the woman. No one was willing to take responsibility for their *own* actions. Imagine that!

If you are addicted to alcohol and you are reading this section of my book, take a moment and look within. Many addicts blame God, they blame their upbringing; their parents, their spouses and the list goes on. Believe me, there is plenty of blame to go around. Perhaps, you were raised in the wrong neighborhood, so society is to blame? Or maybe, you didn't get that job that you had applied for, or the last ten jobs you applied for. These disappointments in life can weigh heavily on anyone and you are not alone.

Ellaina's Story:

The Wrecking Ball of Abuse

One day I, my younger sister, my brother and my dad went and got a loaded shotgun that had 6 bullets in it. There were 6 shot glasses lined up, and his plan was to shoot all of us, one shot glass for each of us. A knock on the door from my older brother, praise God, stopped our would be fate of killing each of us then ultimately plan on taking his own life. I was ten years old and I was old enough to understand something bad would happen. Praise God we were spared that day.

Scriptures to Ponder:

"We destroy arguments and every lofty opinion raised against the knowledge of God, and take every thought captive to obey Christ." 2 Corinthians 10:5 ESV

"Finally, brothers, whatever is true, whatever is honorable, whatever is just, whatever is pure, whatever is lovely, whatever is commendable, if there is any excellence, if there is anything worthy of praise, think about these things." Philippians 4:8 ESV

Conclusion

Be Positive at All Times!

Bottom line, negativity in totality involves a war going on in the mind. This threat to your mental health is multiplied when you are addicted or are the family member or caregiver of someone addicted to alcohol. Remember the scene that we read earlier, was being played out in the Garden? Well, this is what happens on an ongoing basis. There is a war going on in your head and with your permission. When the enemy tries to speak to you, put negative thoughts in your mind, you have the power to stop this.

Read the scriptures throughout this book and memorize those that you identify most with, as you go through the road to recovery. Read them out loud, they have a powerful effect when read out loud to stop the voice of satan and to magnify the power of God. But there is one major ingredient; you must have faith to believe God's word has power over the enemy's attack on your thoughts. Scriptures are powerful because they are from God and can overthrow the plans and schemes of the evil one. Don't ever doubt this for one minute. God's word works.

You are almost at the finish line, keep reading further and don't ever give up.

CHAPTER SEVEN

The Guilt Factor

[There is] therefore now no condemnation to them which are in Christ Jesus, who walk not after the flesh, but after the Spirit. Romans 8:1 (KJV)

There was a young man named Daniel requested to be among many children who go through a period of preparation to go before the King. During that time of preparation, they were to eat special food and drink choice wine (strong drink) from the King's prime delectable.

However, Daniel refused to partake of the King's choice foods, as a young man he understood the importance to avoid over consumption of food and wine. He knew the ramifications of being drunk; failure to be sober minded could result in his inability to serve God. He understood his prophetic gift as a dreamer and the assignment on his life. Daniel understood if he did not remain sober, he could miss God and as a result miss out on the good future God had planned for his life. For the most part, Daniel knew strong drink would pollute his body and redirect his fate. Fortunately, God showed Himself strong in Daniel's life and he did not miss God, but was able to go on to be a force to be reckoned with by not bowing to the realm of darkness; yet overcome evil by the hand of God on his life.

And the king appointed them a daily provision of the king's meat, and of the wine which he drank: so nourishing them three years, that at the end thereof they might stand before the king. *Now among these were of the children of Judah, Daniel, Hananiah, Mishael, and Azariah:*

Unto whom the prince of the eunuchs gave names: for he gave unto Daniel the name of Belteshazzar; and to Hananiah, of Shadrach; and to Mishael, of Meshach; and to Azariah, of Abednego.

But Daniel purposed in his heart that he would not defile himself with the portion of the king's meat, nor with the wine which he drank: therefore he requested of the prince of the eunuchs that he might not defile himself.

Suffering in Silence

Many people who become addicted to alcohol find themselves suffering in a world of silence. They hide bottles from people who are close to them and family members. For a period of time, they often live beneath the shadow of glass bottles and under the radar of drinking alone in conjunction with the scenes of a normal life. Family members also live under the auspice of the quiet storm brewing beneath the surface, often walking on eggshells while watching the one they love, seemingly drifting away into the deep dark waters of a drunken stupor.

The clues often follow expressions of denial, no one is willing to discuss a situation that they refuse to discuss. Facing the truth in an unstable environment can be uncomfortable as well as inconsistent, balancing the truth with the hidden lies under the surface of the problem.

Below are a few clues to be aware of in order to understand the signs that someone is hiding bottles. Alcoholics are often dishonest about their problem, especially when they are going through the early stages of recovery. Another thing, they may just shut down when confronted about their drinking problem, especially when they are not quite ready to face the ugly honest truth.

5 Clues to recognize your loved one may be drinking behind the scenes:

- You notice the smell of alcohol on their breath or they may try to mask the odor with cough drops, breath mints and mouth wash.
- They act suspicious when you walk in the room.
- They would rather spend time alone at home and often turn down social invites or make excuses to avoid attending family events.
- They act strangely when you bring up the subject of drinking and would rather not, "talk about it."
- They avoid responsibility and often blame their problems on everyone else accept themselves.

Check out the following:

5 Steps to take below when the signs are right under your nose.

Don't ignore them, and take fast action to get the necessary help required as soon as possible. Do not delay.

- Recognize abuse and don't ignore the truth hidden in front of you.
- Be aware of the sudden changes, especially the "subtle" changes, most people miss.
- Confrontation is the best option, not the last option.
- Remember love is not always easy, but always operating in love is necessary.
- Act bold and act quickly, make the changes necessary in order to stop this disease in its tracks.

Disassociate with all Toxic Relationships in Your Life NOW!!!!

Toxicity is poison; it can clog the arteries of your life. Relationships are supposed to be uplifting, edifying and exciting. Family, friends, co-workers and associates can cause your life to spiral out of control, especially when they are toxic. Toxicity can cause your entire life to become contaminated. Remember in the beginning of this chapter, we read about Daniel? Well, Daniel understood the importance of not blending in with the crowd. He knew that separation from toxic food, strong drink and even unbelievers was the best option for having optimal success in life.

Sometimes in order to have a "clean slate" having full control over your choice of friends, food, and drink will propel you to a better future. Making the wrong choices in either of these areas, can place you on a roller coaster ride; experiencing sickness, suffering and ultimately soul searching for solutions to problems that could have been avoided.

A life full of fighting, arguing and full of drama will cause mental stress and in some cases, physical decline.

Some effects of alcohol on the body include:

- *Kidney disease and failure*
- *Liver cirrhosis*
- *Pancreatitis*
- *Bad breath*
- *Risk for falls*
- *Altered Central Nervous System*
- *Loss of focus*
- *Slurred speech*
- *Loss of Memory*
- *Depression*
- *Stomach and digestion issues*
- *Blood toxicity and Overdose*

The above is a short list of common problems caused by overindulgence. Now you can understand why Daniel abstained from strong drink as well as taking full responsibility of his own destiny.

Happiness comes from within, not outside of oneself. Most people look for everything inside of people, places or things connected to them, instead of searching inside themselves. Everything you need has been placed inside of you. It is time to start looking for what's been there all along. Your success is inside of you! Your happiness is deep within; seeking there to find your answers.

Remember, you absolutely deserve happiness, but happiness begins with you.

Ellaina's Story:

Taking My First Drink

I believed I was next (the next to die after my sister's death). The first time I tasted alcohol it left a strong aftertaste in my mouth. It felt good going down, but that was the beginning of deception. I know now, I would have been next. Yes I did drink as well, but after seeing my sister in the hospital, I was changed. I knew I had to get help, and my older sister basically threatened my life if I did not get help. Drinking really took the pain away after seeing two sisters die much too young.

Scriptures to Ponder:

Happy [is] the man [that] findeth wisdom, and the man [that] getteth understanding. Proverbs 3:13 KJV

He shall deliver thee in six troubles: yea, in seven there shall no evil touch thee. Job 5:19 KJV

Conclusion

Be Responsible for YOU!

Responsibility over self is more powerful than having responsibility over others, especially when control is the motive. The direct opposite of responsibility is culpability which is very much the same as having a feeling of guilt, but lacking the character to take full responsibility for one's actions. Being responsible is one of the first steps to take to becoming free of addiction. Anything less, would continue the perpetual roller coaster ride of the actions surrounding a life full of toxicity and full of drama. Alcoholism is a terrible distraction to productive families, living life to the fullness filled with joy and peace that can only be found in Jesus Christ, who is the King of Peace.

CHAPTER EIGHT

Selfishness to Recovery

The glory of this present house will be great-er than the glory of the former house,' says the Lord Almighty. 'And in this place I will grant peace,' declares the Lord Almighty."
Haggai 2:9 KJV

In the previous chapter, we discussed the need of the alco-holic to live in seclusion and hide their addiction, but in this chapter, we will discuss how to expose what has been done in secret. It is time to reveal those hidden things done for sometimes for selfish reasons. It is time to move forward and go from a position of selfishness to a posture of recovery.

Haggai was a prophet to the Nation of Israel and spoke on God's behalf to His people during a time period when the nation was controlled by a spirit of greed and the peo-ple were corrupted.

Even though the people were defiled, God told Haggai to tell them He was going to bless them even in their posture of disobedience because he desired to show himself to them once again as a God of LOVE, GRACE and FORGIVENESS. During this period, as usual the people were followers and lived by their emotions and their feelings. But nevertheless, God wanted the people to understand he was with them.

"This is what the Lord Almighty says: 'In a little while I will once more shake the heavens and the earth, the sea and the dry land. 7I will shake all nations, and what is desired by all nations will come, and I will fill this house with glory,' says the Lord Almighty. Haggai 2:6-7

Often times when alcoholics are going through the symptoms of recovery, everyone around them is also going through a time of shaking and a time of withdrawals. This period seems to never end. But God wants you to know, you are not alone. He is always near. Just as he told the Israelites time and time again, during their seasons of selfishness, due to their times of withdrawal from God's presence and posture of self-sabotage by the spirit of greed.

Most Addicts Don't Believe They Are Selfish.

Selfishness is a symptom of GREED. According to Merriam-Webster.com, Greed is defined as a selfish and excessive desire for more of something (as money) than is needed. Greed is a spirit of anonymity, that most people who suffer in the silence of addiction, or those who cover for them (aid and abet) their problem, don't really understand the full gravity of their position in their loved one's life.

You can break free! Let's discuss below the following six ways to break free from selfishness and move towards recovery once and for all.

1. **Think for yourself**- Stop allowing people to control your thoughts. You understand right from wrong, so think independently and make bold choices to become positive. Loving and giving instead of selfish, full of greed and putting your own needs above everyone else.

2. **Forgiveness starts with you**- Forgiveness starts with you making a step forward towards change. Change will never come looking for you, instead, you have to go looking for change. Read, research, and empower yourself by finding the answers to your problems. Stop making people do your dirty work, free them from the net of selfishness that has them intertwined in your addiction.

3. **Detoxify**- Cleanse your mind! Our minds are filled with trauma from our past. Your mind must be cleansed by reading the word of God. In addition, it is important to cleanse your relationships. If most of your friends drink, family members drink, in order to save your own life remove yourself from negative relationships. People who think like you do may be hazardous to your health.

4. **Sensitivity**- Stop being so sensitive! Everyone is not out to get you. Again, renew your mind with clean thinking and forgive anyone who has offended you. Only when you can forgive others can you receive forgiveness.

5. **Look Within**- Quit it! Quit looking outside of yourself for change and begin to look inside for the change that is already inside of you. Stop blaming others for the decisions you have made, look deep inside and do some soul searching within. Over time, you may discover the hidden treasure you have been keeping to yourself, so begin to share positivity with those you love.

6. **Be Positive**- Positivity is the position of choice. There are two choices in this case, positive or negative. These same two forces are living within every one of us. Therefore, we must choose to be positive, speak positive, and react to problems from a mindset or position of positivity.

Ellaina's Story:

Liquid Courage

Alcohol has a way of tricking you to think you can do things you can never do on your own. I remember going to my sister's house and seeing these bottles that had the appearance of water inside of them. Because you feel like you have to have it at all cost. Alcohol calls your name and you quench its thirst. People don't realize how powerful that first drink can be. Bottles of vodka were everywhere around her house, but one gallon jugs all over her house, filled with vodka. She hid her vodka in water bottles to hide her drinking problems. The great lengths people will go to hide their addiction. What a horrific way to die. Allowing a substance to eat you alive and die a slow painful death.

Scriptures to Ponder:

'But now be strong, Zerubbabel,' declares the Lord. 'Be strong, Joshua son of Jozadak, the high priest. Be strong, all you people of the land,' declares the Lord, 'and work. For I am with you,' declares the Lord Almighty. 'This is what I covenanted with you when you came out of Egypt. And my Spirit remains among you. Do not fear.' Haggai 2:5-6

Conclusion

Time to Break Free!

Remember, breaking free from the selfish disease of alcohol addiction is not an easy feat by anyone's perspective, but it can be done. Many people have been loosened from the grip of addiction and have gone on to live a prosperous life. The six steps I shared above may seem a bit harsh initially, but if you take the initiative to work on these areas, you will be on the road to living a positive life, free of selfishness and free from the entrapment in a net filled with drama draining people and toxic family relationships.

Start with you, look within and get to know yourself all over again. Once the cloud of alcohol induced forgetfulness wears off comes clarity and unfortunately self-discovery of who you are, who you hurt, and the consequences of years of shameful choices. Don't get caught in the web of guilt, but forgive yourself as often as required and take the necessary precautions to walk in the newness of who you really are on the inside.

CHAPTER NINE

It's Not Your Fault-Reprogramming

*"Therefore if any man be in Christ, he is a new
creature: old things are passed away; behold,
all things are become new." 2 Corinthians 5:17*

Now is the time to take a bold look within, and face your
own demon. The best way to take this bold step forward
is to plan time for yourself. Be alone, Yes let me repeat,
be alone. Most enablers find this step to be more difficult, but there is no way around getting to know yourself
again. Stop self-inflicting wounds of repeating your faults
over and over again. Once you decide to look inside, stop
feeling guilty and being ashamed of what you have tol-
erated for so long. Now is the time to face the facts and
move ahead, no looking back.

Giving your life to Jesus is the first step to reprogram-
ming your life, and turning away from your past mistakes.
God has forgiven you and now it is time you forgive your-

self. Beginning to think for yourself is another first step. Thinking for yourself is your right, so stop meandering through life walking on egg shells. This time, safety precautions permit you serving yourself first. When on an airplane the stewardess always tells the adult to place the oxygen mask on themselves first and then assist the child or the dependent person next to them. Now this is your time to get to the boat, rescue yourself first before you can help others. Now is the time for you to get your mind set on first priorities. You are your first priority.

REPROGRAM YOUR MIND

Forgiveness begins with you, and after you can successfully forgive yourself, then accept forgiveness from Jesus, only after these steps will you be able to forgive those around you. God has forgiven your past sins, and therefore your sins are forgiven. Accept the truth and leave the prison of self-hate and selfishness. Ask God for help, and He will answer. *1 John Chapter 1:9 says, "If we confess our sins, he is faithful and just to forgive us our sins, and to cleanse us from all unrighteousness."* Remember this comes with no conditions except God's love and don't depend on your feelings, depend on His word. If God's word says it, then that settles it. You are forgiven.

IT'S TIME TO DETOX!

Detoxification can be done in many ways. But in this book I will share ways to detoxify through living a fasting life. A fasting life involves fasting food, drink and substances. Fasting means "abstaining" or living without particular objects or subjects of choice over a period of time. *Jesus fasted for 40 days and 40 nights from food and water as noted in the Bible, Matthew 4:2 After he fasted forty days and forty nights, he was famished... Jesus did not eat anything for 40 days and 40 nights. At the end of that time, he was hungry...*

Listen, I am not suggesting you fast this extensive period as Jesus did, and in the event you fast any substance, especially food or water, please seek medical advice. Remember, I am not a medical doctor or mental health professional. So please seek advice from a professional before following any proposal in this book. My goal is to only share ideas that have worked for myself and others that I have encountered over time.

Other folks I know have abstained from going to the movies, social media, technology, books, phone, or whatever keeps them from being in the presence of God and concentrating on prayer or meditation. This also has been a significant journey to change. Others have chosen to dabble in their gifts or talents and share them with the community or work interest. Pampering yourself is also a positive way to relax and detox your mind, body and soul.

REPROGRAM YOUR MIND

Detox your body from the outside by getting a full body message, facial and reflexology. Exercise your body and mind by reading your Bible, self-help books like this one, yoga class or join a support meet-up group like the ones listed below.

- *Bible Study*
- *Divorce Care*

- *Therapy Guided Support*
- *Alcoholics Anonymous*
- *Al-Anon*

Many times detoxing from certain people helps immensely. Staying in the wrong circle of friends can and will set you back if you remain in the same place mentally or physically. Television can be a culprit as well. Be careful of what you watch on television. Stop allowing negativity to loop around in your head. Watch what you allow your mind to concentrate on. Thinking positively takes discipline. We have to exercise our mind, just as we exercise our bodies. Spending time with positive people will help. Before long you will begin to grab or hold to those negative thoughts and take them captive.

Lastly, find a mentor. Positive mentors and role models help in guiding your life and steering you in the right direction. Mentors have wisdom and can often notice the signs in you that may take you off focus. A mentor can quickly place you back on the right track to a positive life.

SET YOUR BOUNDARIES

Below are a few ways to take care of yourself while you are going through your mind-shift. Remember a mind shift can take a while for some and for others, God can make a quick change. The difference is, are you willing to change? Are you ready to let go and let God do a new work in you and change you? If so, get ready for an amazing LIFE!

- Take care of yourself- It's ok to take care of yourself. Do YOU?

- Recover- A snap back or bouncing back can be as easy as saying, I'm sorry, or forgive me. Just that simple!

- Mind shift- Allow your mind to think differently. Stop seeing the glass half empty and begin to see it half full. Instead of seeing lemons, make a tall glass of lemonade.

- Changing behaviors-No more sitting on the couch at home alone, get up, get out and exercise, go on vacation, take a long drive. Have dinner with friends. No more drinking!

- Feel Your Feelings-The pat on the back you are looking for may never come, but look past the pain and face your own feelings. Stop allowing takers to take advantage of you.

- Disown Old Feelings-Stop all the EXCUSES. Always seeking Validation/Blames on Me/its runs in my family/whose agenda is it?

- INSAINTY? Stop it!-The definition of insanity is to keep doing the same thing, over and over and over, expecting the a different outcome. Stop it!

- Learn how to say NO and mean it-Let your yes be YES and your no be NO!

- No more PEOPLE pleasing!-Stop trying to please everyone. Remember this is your time. It's ok to be self-caring, self-loving and self-nurturing.

Ellaina's Story:

A Fork in the Road

I will never forget the counselor asking me, Well, how is your way working? What's the alternative? Give me a few weeks of your life and watch God. My older sister had heard about a guy in my church who had helped a lot of people. He was a former football player, who had a great anointing on him like the Apostle Paul. I knew I needed to stop drinking, although I did not feel I was addicted at all, during this time I was, however, hurting after the loss of both of my sisters back to back.

Scriptures to Ponder:

But Jesus beheld them and said unto them, with men this is impossible; but with God all things are possible. Matthew 19:26

For with God nothing shall be impossible. Luke 1:37

I can do all things through Christ which strengthens me. Philipians 4:13

Conclusion:

Block TOXIC People!

Pressure or anxiety happens because we fail to see the big picture. FEAR is the main reason most people fall into the traps of co-dependency and alcohol or drug abuse in the first place. Instigators are people you must stay far from in order to get YOUR LIFE BACK! Be very cautious about who you share your information with. Remember everyone cannot be trusted with the details of your life, especially your recovery. Sharing information with the wrong person can set you back if they decide to DECODE you and use that negative information against you.

Again, block toxic people, places and things! Sounds really easy, but this can be the change that trumps every other advice in this book. Trusting a few people in your close inner circle is absolutely ok, such as your mentor or close friend, a spouse or co-worker; but keep the circle real close. Lastly, slow down and give your DESTINY time to catch up with God's plan that is specially tailored and ordained for you. Patience is the KEY.

CHAPTER TEN

Mind Mastery

Let this MIND be in YOU, which is also in Christ Jesus.
Philipians 2:5 (KJV)

Alcohol and substance abuse affects the mind of everyone involved, including close family members, caretakers and friends. In earlier chapters we discussed trauma, sin and abuse that weigh heavily on the minds and the hearts of everyone concerned. There is a saying that the mind is the "devil's playground" or other sayings such as the "devil made me do it". But no matter who is to blame for your situation or condition, God has a remedy and His name is Jesus. Jesus is the answer to all of the ills of your personal life and those lives you are concerned about.

Read the account below of an example of how God will send us help when we are going through a situation just when we need it the most.

The Lord grant mercy to the household of Onesiphorus, for he often refreshed me, and was not ashamed of my chain; but when he arrived in Rome, he sought me out very zealously and found me. The Lord grant to him that he may find mercy from the Lord in that Day—and you know very well how many ways he ministered to me at Ephesus. 2 Timothy 1 Chapter 1:16-18

There was a man in the Bible (*2 Timothy 3:16-18*) named Onesiphorus. Apostle Paul in his letter to Timothy, made special mention of him because he had refreshed him while staying in his house, "in spite of my chains." This caring fellow was not ashamed of Apostle Paul's *so-called chains.* However the Bible did not mention what kind of chains or affliction Paul was dealing with. Perhaps, it was a particular sin like over eating, over drinking or substance abuse or sexual sins. Could it be whether Paul had a disease? No, not any of the above, Paul was merely speaking of being a prisoner of The Gospel and *wearing the heavy chains* that compels him to preach even under difficult conditions and circumstances.

But on the other hand, many of you reading this book are wearing chains of the aforementioned, such as being chained to someone who is dealing with a problem that you did not cause, but you have to bare those same chains in spite of. Look, you are not alone and just as Onesiphorus refreshed Paul, God will send someone to refresh you! Not only has he sent His Son Jesus to suffer "for us" by taking on our infirmity and trespasses so we don't have to, but he will send you a friend, family member, minister or a mentor to help you and refresh you, relieving you and giving you rest for your soul!

They will seek you out as God places a burden on their hearts to help you, and that is just the way He cares for us, personally until we are strong and whole again!

THINK LIKE CHRIST!

God has created man in his image and in His likeness, so as a result, we must put on the mind of Christ! Repeat after me… "I have the mind of Christ!" The mind is one of the compartments of the inner soul of every human being God has created. If we are going to overcome any kind of chemical abuse or co-dependency of people who are users and abusers, we must begin to THINK like Jesus! God gave us the ability to do this by leaving his WORD and Holy Spirit with us in this place the Bible calls "The World."

Jesus said in *John 16:33, These things I have spoken unto you, that in me ye might have peace. In the world ye shall have tribulation: but be of good cheer; I have overcome the world.*

Allow me to explain, as children of God, we may face all kinds of troubles, but Jesus promises us, He has already overcome them on our behalf and in Him we are always victorious! Praise God!

Once you begin to read the Bible more and more, understand what it says about you, pray every day, attend a local body of believers and most of all stay in the company of sober minded people, you will always remain FREE! This is how we master our minds, our bodies and our spirits! Being with the right people of God determines 90% of happiness and the remaining 10% depends on your ability to desire to change emotionally, psychologically, spiritually and last but not least, physically.

THE TRUTH SHALL SET YOU FREE

The Truth is always in Jesus Christ! Understanding His death was not in vain, but He died for you! Healing comes with the benefits of knowing Him! Do you really want to be healed and set free? Then give up that handicap identification card and walk in boldness with healing and forgiveness in Christ Jesus!

Ellaina's Story:

The Pivotal Moment

There is a time in your life when you have to chose, life or death. Destiny is always calling your name, but alcohol has a way of destroying the lives of those who are hurting. Personally, I had to chose between LIGHT and darkness and the choice is always there. Because Holy Spirit is a gentleman, He will not force Himself on you. In my case, the responsibility was mine and I had to make that decision on my own.

Scriptures to Ponder:

"Thy Word have I hidden in my heart, that I may not sin against thee." Psalms 119:11

For who hath known the mind of the Lord, that he may instruct him? But we have the mind of Christ. 1 Corinthians 2:16

Incline your ear and hear the words of the wise, and apply your heart to my knowledge;

For it is pleasant if you keep them within you; Let them be fixed upon your lips,

So that your trust may be in the Lord; I have instructed you today, even you. Proverbs 22:17-19

Conclusion:

Let God Clean Out Your Closets!

Some people have very disorganized closets that are often full of old junk, clothing, pictures and other memorabilia from years and years gone by. I even know people with clothes in their closets that range from 2-4 dress sizes after years of yo-yo dieting. They often repeat the same ole line saying, "I am going to lose weight again and I will be able to fit into that pair of pants or dress someday." But for many of these people, someday never comes, so they keep old clothes that don't fit and memories that make them feel sad and depressed. Do you want to know what their problem is? I am glad you asked. They have a *soul congestion, and a brain overload!* These people are hoarders of information, memories and yes, old stuff that continue to clutter their mind (soul).

It's time to allow God to clean out the closet of your soul!

We often allow JUNK to go in, but for some, that same junk remains forever, and never goes out! Now is the time to clean out your closet of your mind. Put in God's word daily and over time, you will discover your mind (soul) will be so full of Him and His word, no more things or people will be able to take up room in your mind anymore! Let go of the old stuff and make room for a fresh, clean, NEW Life!

Wrap Up
It's Only the Beginning

And He said to her, "Daughter, your faith has made you well; go in peace and be healed of your affliction. Mark 5:34 (NASB)

And He said unto him, Arise, go thy way: thy faith hath made thee whole. Luke 17:19

On many occasions in scripture, Jesus healed those who had sickness and infirmity in their bodies and on every occasion Jesus healed them according to their own (level) of faith. Once He healed them, he often gave them nearly the same instructions and on both occasions in the scenarios listed above, He commanded them to GO!

BE, WHOLE AGAIN!

He is saying the same to you reading this book today, yes it is time to go on your way and walk in wholeness.

Many of you did not start off the way you see your-self now, each one of us began our journey with the same humble beginnings at birth. But somewhere along the way, we ended up on different paths for different purpos-es only God knows how, when, where we will be at the end of our own personal journeys.

God created us and designed us for greatness, never-theless, as long as we hang on to His unchanging hand, we will arrive at our specific destinations right on time!

Faith is really knowing who God is and believing He is able to help us and deliver us out of every situation. Faith is also a never ending TRUST factor we are all born with a level in us, but only the trials and test of life try us in the fire and refines us until we are shaped perfectly and honed into the quality jewel He desires. None of us are the same, but all of us have a PURPOSE!

Fire purifies us, but God sets the temperature for each of us because He knows how much we are able to handle. But remember, He never leaves us alone in the fire, He is right there withstanding or buffering the heat, holding us in His hands the entire time. Stay in His hands!

Self-Assessment Exercise

Below is an informal exercise that may help you under-stand your relationship to alcohol better. Remember this is a sample exercise and is by no means a way of deter-mining a diagnosis nor will if provide a cure. Please seek medical attention if you need help with overcoming any addiction or abuse. (The author is not responsible for any results or outcome of using this assessment.)

A self-assessment is merely explained as looking within to gain insight about ones self and making a decision to stay the same or change.

Ask yourself the following questions. There are no right or wrong answers.

1. Does your work or home life suffer because of your drinking?
2. Do you use alcohol to mask your true feelings or hide your true identity?
3. Do you use alcohol to boost your mood or confidence?
4. Do you have to drink early in the morning to perk yourself up before starting your day?
5. Are you a social drinker or do your drink alone and hide your bottles around the house?
6. Does drinking cause a drastic unusual change in your behavior, mood or personality?
7. Does your drinking result in legal trouble?
8. Does your drinking cause others in your life to become angry or upset with you?
9. Does your drinking cause your children, spouse or loved ones to become sad or unhappy?
10. Do you tend to over drink or drink obsessively on a regular basis?

If you answered yes to one or more of the questions above, please seek help from a pastor, counselor and/or medical doctor as soon as possible. (Source-http://www.alcoholic.org)

Affirmations (speak these out loud each day and believe!)

– I have the MIND of Christ.

- God Loves me and I am forgiven, no matter how I feel.
- I am the child of the Most High!
- My Destiny will be fulfilled no matter what!
- I am more than a conqueror through Christ Jesus!
- Jesus is always with me, He will never leave me nor forsake me!
- I am covered and protected by God!
- Jesus is my Strong Tower. I run to Him and am safe!
- I am prosperous. I am rich. I am whole and complete in Him!
- I am no longer bound! I am FREE!
- I walk in LOVE! Love covers a multitude of sins.

Resources

Local and National Hotlines

24 Hour Confidential Hotline
713-473-2801
1800-799-SAFE

Christians in Recovery

Email- http://www.fbp.org
Contact-Bobby Grimes

Homeless Shelters for Woman and Children

The Bridge Over Troubled Waters
24-Hour Emergency Hotline: 713-473-2801
Administration: 713-472-0753
Email: thebridge@tbotw.org
The Bridge Over Troubled Waters: 3811 Allen Genoa
Rd, Pasadena, Texas 77504

Houston Women's Centers
713-528-2121

Homeless Shelters for Men & Women

Star of Hope Mission
Website: http://www.sohmission.org
Phone: 713-748-0700
Address: 6897 Ardmore St, Houston, Texas 77054

Additional Resources

Grief Share
Email: http://www.griefshare.org

Divorce Care

Email: http://www.divorcecare.org

Substance Abuse

Alcoholics Anonymous
Phone: 713-686-6300
Al-Anon
Phone: 713-683-7227

Career & Recovery and Drug Treatment (Outpatient)

Phone: 713-754-7000

Domestic Issues

Family Law Hotline
Phone: 1800-777-FAIR (3247)

Family Violence

1800-373- HOPE (4673)

Houston Volunteers Lawyers Intake

General Information
713-228-0732
713-228-0735

Aid-to-Abuse
713-528-2121

Find a Bible Faith Teaching Church in your area and attend regularly.

Do not forsake the assembling of ourselves together, as the manner of some is; but exhorting one another; and so much the more, as ye see the day approaching. Hebrews 10:25

Meet the Author

*"I believe every chapter in life has a closing and new begin-
nings are the amazing paths life has to offer." Ellaina Nicholette Dolater*

*Ellaina has over eight years of experience in leadership.
She continues to motivate men and women through dynam-
ic motivational public speaking as a Cosmetology instructor
and trainer.*

*Ellaina's demanding professional career keeps her busy an
Owner of Spa, Facilitator, and an Ordained Minister.*

The Sinners Prayer
(Prayer of Salvation)

"Father, I know that I have broken your laws and my sins have separated me from you. I am truly sorry, and now I want to turn away from my past sinful life toward you. Please forgive me, and help me avoid sinning again. I believe that your son, Jesus Christ died for my sins, was resurrected from the dead, is alive, and hears my prayer. I invite Jesus to become the Lord of my life, to rule and reign in my heart from this day forward. Please send your Holy Spirit to help me obey you, and to do your will for the rest of my life. In Jesus' name I pray, Amen." (Source: KingJamesBibleVerses.com)

Made in the USA
San Bernardino, CA
16 March 2017